Original title:
Parallel Planet Puns

Copyright © 2025 Creative Arts Management OÜ
All rights reserved.

Author: Adeline Fairfax
ISBN HARDBACK: 978-1-80567-808-3
ISBN PAPERBACK: 978-1-80567-929-5

Universes Untangled

In a cosmos where time's a loop,
Aliens dance in a happy group.
One says, 'I'm from a place so neat,
Where pizza's round and the pies can't be beat.'

In my world, the cows jump high,
Wearing jetpacks, they soar the sky.
They moo to tunes of the latest hit,
And have a dance-off, just for a bit.

Stars of Similar Spheres

Two suns shine bright, not quite the same,
One's all hot, the other's a game.
They race in orbit, just for fun,
While shooting stars play hide and run.

Galaxies giggle, swirling in lines,
Making faces with twisty designs.
The black holes fart, they pull with might,
Creating laughter with every bite.

Twin Tales from the Cosmos

A duo of twins from a distant star,
One flew high while the other sank far.
They swapped their places, what a fuss,
One liked silence, the other loved fuss!

At dinner time, they'd joke and tease,
Eating moon pies with cosmic cheese.
They'd argue who's faster, with a wink,
One says, 'I zoom, you barely blink!'

Asteroid Anecdotes

In a field of rocks circling round,
Asteroids play catch with no sound.
One joked, 'I'm shaped like a shoe!'
'You're just mad that your rock's not blue!'

They roll and spin, a cosmic game,
Telling stories of space, oh so lame.
A comet zips by with a wink and a smile,
Says, 'Don't rush, take a cosmic while!'

Celestial Echoes

In a galaxy where laughs collide,
Stars trade jokes, no need to hide.
Comets fly with punchlines bright,
Nebulas giggle in the night.

Planets bounce in cosmic cheer,
Asteroids whisper, lend an ear.
Aliens chuckle, space suits tight,
Gravity drags on jokes just right.

Galactic Giggles

Black holes spiral in laughter's grip,
While moons spin tales and never trip.
Saturn's rings are just gold bling,
Mars tells tales of one cool fling.

Quasars blink, their signals strong,
Echoing laughter in a cosmic song.
Starships zoom through punchy skies,
In this universe, humor never dies.

Two Worlds, One Punchline

Earth and Mars share jokes by day,
While Venus laughs in a cheeky way.
Uranus says, 'I'm humor's host!'
While Neptune serves a cosmic roast.

Two worlds twist in humor's dance,
Creating memes from a single chance.
Astro comedians, they take the stage,
In the solar system, they turn the page.

Double Duty in the Cosmos

Stars take shifts in the cosmic joke,
While planets nod and gently poke.
Asteroids act as a funny guide,
Through the universe, we all slide.

Satellites scurry, laughter they bring,
Orbiting in a light-hearted swing.
Witty comets race through the air,
In this vast space, there's joy to share.

Cosmic Kinship Quips

In the Milky Way cafe, stars sip tea,
Jupiter jokes, 'I'm so big, can't you see?'
Mars flips a red coin, calls heads or tails,
While comets speed by, sharing their tales.

Uranus winks shyly, says he's not round,
Saturn comments, 'Great rings I have found!'
Venus then giggles, 'Why not dance a jig?'
With laughter echoing, all planets dig.

Mercury zips past with a pun in flight,
'Why did the sun take a nap last night?'
The whole solar system bursts into glee,
As they orbit around this joke jubilee.

Neptune shouts, 'What's a planet's best friend?'
'A comet, of course, that trails to the end!'
Galaxies twinkle, while black holes amass,
In this cosmic joke, we all come to pass.

Starlit Silhouettes

In a dance of dark nights, starlight beams,
Pulsars chuckle about dying dreams.
While black holes gulp stars, a gluttonous feat,
The moons make a plan to host a sweet treat.

'Throw a bash,' yells Pluto, with humor intact,
'Let's gather the orbs for a cosmic pact!'
'Bring snacks!' calls out Neptune, with a grin,
'And make sure they're orbiting, let the feast begin.'

Mars brings spicy chips, full of heat,
While Venus serves drinks that can't be beat.
Galaxy giggles fill up the space,
As shooting stars scatter, setting the pace.

Light years apart but close at heart,
These celestial friends have perfected the art.
With laughter they twirl in a starry ballet,
Creating horizons where puns bloom and play.

Interplanetary Punchlines

A Martian with laughter once said to the Moon,
'Your face is so bright, you'll eclipse us by noon!'
The Sun rolled its eyes, shook with delight,
'You don't get burned by puns, just by my light!'

Venus chimed in, 'What's swirling in space?
A cow giving milk at a cosmic pace!'
Jupiter laughed loud, thumping his chest,
'In this joke galaxy, we are truly blessed!'

Mercury zips round, sharing wit so fast,
'Why don't comets get lost in the past?'
Saturn rolled its rings, gleaming with cheer,
'The answer's in orbit, it's really quite clear.'

Amidst the stardust, joy takes its reign,
With humor unbound, a light-hearted chain.
Planets unite in celestial fun,
In laughter and light, they shine like the sun.

Universes of Uproar

Beyond the Milky Way, there's a planet with flair,
Where aliens gather, trading puns in the air.
One zany being asked with a grin,
'Is your salad from space? Because it's out of this bin!'

The crowd erupted, with echoes of cheer,
While meteors sped, delivering good beer.
A starship captain smirked, 'Let's launch a show,'
To tickle constellations and make laughter grow.

From Virgo to Orion, jesters are found,
Each punchline goes cosmic, echoing sound.
While light-years tick by, the fun won't run dry,
'What did the black hole say?' they ask with a sigh.

'Can't see the jokes, they vanish too fast,
But don't worry, my friends, they're bound to outlast!'
In vastness of giggles, the stars twinkle bright,
Creating a universe filled with delight.

Orbiting Oddities

Two spheres spin in tight embrace,
One drinks coffee, the other laces.
In this cosmos, jesters play,
While moons do cartwheels in dismay.

One moon forgot to wear a shoe,
The other jokes, 'That's quite the view!'
Stars chuckle while they align,
Orbiting tales of cosmic wine.

Simultaneous Stardust

Galaxies giggle, a cosmic joke,
Planets popping, like well-blown smoke.
One star sings in a silly tune,
While comets dance like a cartoon.

Wormholes wink with a cheeky tease,
Galactic gnomes planting space trees.
Nebulas shimmer, pranks in the air,
In their twinkling, a grand affair.

Alternative Astral Adventures

In a realm where time's a riddle,
Planets play a tune, quite diddle.
A sun that's shy, it blinks and hides,
While moons engage in cheeky rides.

One planet swears it's made of cheese,
The other giggles, 'What a tease!'
Stars paint escapades on the sky,
With cosmic jokes that never die.

Doppelplanets in Dissonance

Two worlds clash in a jestful scene,
One loves to sketch, the other to glean.
Satellites spin with glee and delight,
As orbits twist in a playful fight.

This planet bakes, and that one fries,
Their food fights draw curious eyes.
In a vacuum, laughter resonates,
For cosmic pranks, oh, how it rates!

Cosmic Comedy Carousel

In a starry diner up in space,
Aliens joke with wide-eyed grace.
Sipping tea from mugs made of cheese,
They laugh 'til their sides ache, if you please.

A comet joked, 'I'm on a roll!',
While black holes shared their portal goal.
Gravity's got a heavy punchline,
Sending punchlines towards the divine.

When Martians twirl with laughter bright,
Their dances spark in the cosmic night.
A moonlight jig, spinning with glee,
Shadows of Saturn join in, carefree.

Uranus chortles with giant mirth,
Tickling stars, twisting their girth.
In this giggle galaxy, joy's the wealth,
Each chuckle shared boosts the health.

Interstellar Irony

In a comet's tail, a lost shoe lies,
'Hope you don't trip under starry skies!'
An asteroid shrugged and winked with flair,
'At least I've got space to spare!'

A nebula poured over punchline soup,
Sharing jokes in a cosmic loop.
Stars jokingly burn with envy and cheer,
While planets groan at their own frontiers.

On Jupiter's lap, a riddle sat,
'What did the sun say to the cat?'
That feline meowed, 'You're much too bright!'
And winked at Venus, catching delight.

Black holes snicker, pulling in the jest,
Wondering who's really the best.
A supernova snapped with zest,
Leaving laughter in the universe's chest.

Etherial Humor

Up in the ether, where laughter swirls,
Galaxies spin with giggly twirls.
A starlet beamed, 'I'm a glowing delight!',
But a dwarf star snorted, 'That's not polite!'

In the void, a cosmic clown juggles dreams,
With cosmic cherries and rainbow beams.
Saturn's rings clink like a laughter bell,
Echoing puns that they know so well.

While Venus blushes at silly quips,
Orbits swirling with comedic flips.
'That Martian's got rocks in his head!'
Giggles erupt, as truth is shed.

Puns float like comets, bright and airy,
In the cosmos, humor's legendary.
With stardust tickles and cosmic grins,
Every journey begins where laughter spins.

Celestial Satirical Soiree

In a space soirée under twinkling light,
Stars gather for jokes of stellar might.
A quasar quipped of the latest craze,
A dance called the 'Galactic Gaze'.

Mars brought Martian meringues to munch,
While asteroids played a celestial punch.
'Why did the sun start wearing shades?'
'To block out the punny charades?'

The rogue planet grinned with sly surprise,
'These Earthlings think they're so wise!'
Yet laughter echoed through the cosmic void,
A harmony that could not be destroyed.

As comets raced with joyfully strange flair,
Their trails shimmered like confetti in air.
Together they basked, in humor's embrace,
A universal joke shared, across time and space.

Twin Tales from Beyond

Two worlds collide, what a sight,
One wears glasses, the other in flight.
They argue who's alien, who's neat,
Yet both think pizza's the best treat.

In one realm, the dogs can talk,
In the other, cats take a walk.
Each day they swap, just for fun,
Debating who'd win a nutty pun.

Space cows moo in countless tones,
While dancing robots chill on phones.
They laugh aloud at cosmic dread,
While ordering doughnuts, fresh and spread.

With tales of quirks that make us grin,
From wacky starts to crazy ends.
These twin tales spin, they never tire,
In a universe that loves to inspire.

Asteroid Antics

Asteroids roll in a cosmic race,
One's got freckles, the other's a case.
They zoom through stars, causing a fuss,
With rock 'n' roll that's made for us.

One asteroid claims to know the vibe,
The other just laughs, it's quite a tribe.
With zany pranks that shake the void,
Each day's a thrill, nothing destroyed.

They paint themselves with craters and dust,
In space, even rocks have to trust.
They swap their paths; no dull routine,
One's a jokester, the other's the queen.

Asteroids clink their mineral cups,
Sipping on stardust, laughing it up.
With every twist, a new jest starts,
These cosmic rocks have brilliant hearts.

Lightyears of Laughter

Traveling far on beams of delight,
Tickling stars in the still of the night.
Galactic giggles echo through space,
As laughter unfolds in a celestial race.

One comet's joke flies with great flair,
Nebulae shimmer, joining the air.
They lighten the load of dark matter's weight,
With puns that only black holes can rate.

Each galaxy grins with radiant beams,
Sharing the wildest of cosmic dreams.
Lightyears stretch, but humor's more fast,
United in laughter, a joy unsurpassed.

So come take a trip, ride a wave of fun,
Where stars joke about the things we shun.
In this vast universe, laughter takes lead,
Making the journey a cosmic creed.

Dimension Driftwood

In a sea of dimensions all askew,
Driftwood floats with quirks new.
It waves at suns, and cheers to the breeze,
With a giggle echoing through the trees.

This wood tells tales of places absurd,
Where fish might chant, and frogs have heard.
Every grain holds a jesting rhyme,
A drift of time in a pit of crime.

Wanderers laugh at its curious form,
Where logic bends and dreams transform.
Each wave tickles truths of the unknown,
In a universe made of giggles, full-grown.

The driftwood whispers of joys untold,
With every ripple a pun unfold.
Jumping dimensions, so carefree and bright,
In this funny wood, everything's right.

Space-time Shenanigans

In a galaxy far away, they bake,
Stars in the oven, make no mistake.
Saturn's rings are a pizza slice,
Jupiter's storms? Just some nice spice.

Time travels back for a laugh,
Black holes just love a good photograph.
Einstein took a selfie, with a twist,
In the cosmos, humor can't be missed.

Light years fly in a wink,
Martians brew chocolate milk to drink.
Asteroids crack jokes, floating near,
In their orbit, there's nothing to fear.

Warp drives spin tales with flare,
In cosmic realms, laughter fills the air.
With every tick of the cosmic clock,
Witty comets give the best schtick.

Nebula Nonsense

A swirling cloud of gas and bright light,
Clouds do the can-can, a hilarious sight.
Constellations do the tango with grace,
In the cosmos, laughter takes its place.

Planets juggle, spinning with delight,
A supernova went shopping last night.
Stars play cards, what a sight to see,
Through the Milky Way, they banter with glee.

Meteor showers rain down some jokes,
Cosmic clowns in their asteroid cloaks.
Galaxies twirl in a dizzying spin,
In the vastness, the fun won't wear thin.

Nebulas burst with laughter and light,
Creating new worlds in a giggly flight.
With each puff of gas, a punchline is born,
In this universe, humor is worn!

Celestial Comedy Club

Welcome to the club, take a seat,
Where the stars tell jokes, oh so sweet.
Mars is the host, with a wink and a smile,
He cracks puns that take a mile.

Venus roasts Earth, it's all in good fun,
Jupiter laughs and says, 'You're number one!'
Pluto's on the mic, gets a cheer,
'I'm still in the club, despite my last year!'

Black holes are bouncers, they pull you inside,
Eclipsing the laughter, their silence won't hide.
Cosmic comedians, a stellar lineup,
With giggles that echo, they never give up.

Saturn brings snacks, rings made of chips,
Nibble away while you enjoy the quips.
In this club above, amid stars we call home,
The jokes never stop, in the great cosmic dome.

Quasar Quips

Radiating light from a distant core,
Quasars make jokes; who could ask for more?
Blinking bright with cosmic flair,
Their laughter travels through endless air.

Angels in their halos start to spin,
Literally a 'light' year to begin.
Neutrinos chuckle as they dance about,
In the universe, there's no doubt.

Spinning tales in a whirlpool of fun,
Gravity laughs, 'I'm never done!'
Across the void, a giggle we hear,
As quasars wink, with a cosmic cheer.

So join the party, across the vast skies,
With beams of humor that light up the eyes.
In the depths of space, where the cosmos nips,
Quasar quips send us into laughter's grips!

Echoes of Ethereal Existence

In a realm where giggles float,
Jokes from stars, oh what a quote!
Galaxies chuckle with delight,
Wink at comets zooming by night.

Martians dance with silly grace,
Juggling moons, a wild race.
Pluto's puns are always grand,
Making quips with icy hands.

Asteroids throw a raucous bash,
Meteor showers, oh what a splash!
In this zone of cosmic jest,
Laughter echoes, never rests.

Cosmic clowns in spacesuits bright,
Twirl through black holes, what a sight!
With each punchline, planets spin,
In this universe, laughs begin.

Lightyear Laughtracks

Zooming past in light's own tune,
Stars giggle under a laughing moon.
Time flies while humor's in the air,
Joyful echoes dance with flair.

Rocket ships, a comic crew,
Chasing dreams, with laughter too.
Wormholes twist, and jokes take flight,
In hyperspace, there's pure delight.

Aliens telling jokes so bad,
Even black holes start to be glad.
Every quasar shares a grin,
In this cosmos, fun can't thin.

So pull the lever, shift the gear,
Shooting for laughter, no time for fear.
In this adventure, joy's the aim,
Across the stars, we play the game.

Celestial Mirth

Stardust sprinkled on a quip,
Galactic giggles make stars skip.
Meteorites with jokes on track,
Spreading laughter, there's no lack.

Neptune's ne'er-do-wells sing a tune,
Singing silly songs to the moon.
Whirling rings of Saturn's cheer,
Tickle your funny bone, so near.

Eclipses hide the punchlines well,
In the shadows, the chuckles swell.
Even the sun can't help but grin,
As light bends where the fun begins.

Cosmic jokes light up the skies,
Where laughter flows and spirit flies.
Each twinkling star with a wink to share,
In this universe, joy's everywhere.

Alternate Axis Antics

In a realm where axes skew,
Funky fables come out of the blue.
Planets spin in a silly dance,
Joking, jumping, down the cosmic prance.

Gravity's lost a weighty bet,
Floating jokes that you won't forget.
In this world of quirky laws,
Everybody's laughing, taking a pause.

Solar flares with humor bright,
Bursts of laughter fill the night.
Mars and Venus trading jests,
On this axis, fun never rests.

Horizons bend, time takes a leap,
As we dive into laughter so deep.
In the universe's grand scheme,
Finding joy is always the dream.

Jokes from the Jupiter Junction

Why did the comet never stop?
It couldn't find a cosmic shop.
With asteroids blocking the lane,
It rolled on, laughing in vain.

Did you hear about the gas giant's band?
Their songs were out of this world, quite grand.
But when they played their final tune,
The stars all laughed, 'What a balloon!'

A meteorite asked a star, 'How's your day?'
The star replied, 'Bright in every way!'
But a satellite chimed in, quite miffed,
'Your shine is fine, but I'm the gift!'

In Jupiter's realm, all jokes collide,
With gravity pulling laughter inside.
Even the moons join in the cheer,
Orbiting fun without any fear.

Fables of the Fractured Firmament

Once a star had a bright idea,
To dance with planets, oh what a spree!
But tripped on some stardust in the night,
Giggled so hard, became a light.

A wise old comet spun a tale,
About a dwarf who tried to sail.
He ended up lost, quite bemused,
Now he just frolics, mildly confused.

The nebula sighed, 'What a show,
With all these characters, we won't go slow.'
It puffed and glimmered, sparks did fly,
Laughter erupted in the cosmic sky.

In skies so vast, all tales are spun,
With fractures that lead to fathomless fun.
Each star and planet, their quirks they share,
Fables echo, they're everywhere!

Exoplanetary Escapades

On an afar world, they play all day,
A robot golfer who can't putt away.
He swings his club into the green,
And thwacks an alien, what a scene!

Two moons debated who shines best,
While a comet popped in for a jest.
'Your glow is nice, but mine's quite cool,'
'You're full of gas!' was the comfy fool.

Spaceships zoom by with squeals of delight,
As aliens cheer from morning 'til night.
They hosted a race across the stars,
But tripped on their feet, 'Ouch, there go the cars!'

In the cosmic swirl where hilarity reigns,
Every adventure leaves behind strange stains.
From joy to chaos, they flip and they flop,
These exoplanet fun times, they never stop.

Spectrum of Similar Settings

In a universe where all seem the same,
Life's little quirks ignite the flame.
Planets stare while comets tease,
'Are we all siblings?' asks the breeze.

One planet's blue, another's gray,
Each spinning merry in their display.
While galaxies twist and giggle in mirth,
Stars share jokes about their birth.

Suns wink slyly, casting rays of fun,
'We might be different, but we all run!'
In the cosmos, humor's the binding thread,
We're all just stardust, happily spread.

So here's to the worlds, diverse and bright,
Each with a laugh that feels just right.
With puns flying high, and laughter so free,
Together we'll shine in this grand spree.

Cosmic Contrast

In a galaxy not far, a star plays tic-tac-toe,
While its twin spins donuts in a cosmic show.
One moon jumps rope, the other takes a nap,
Asteroids crack jokes, in a stardust trap.

A comet once slipped on a rainbow trail,
Its friend laughed so hard, it turned bright pale.
Wormholes are often just time's silly pranks,
Echoes of laughter in space's empty banks.

Nebulae bloom like cosmic flowers bright,
As suns compete for the best light fight.
Constellations giggle in their starry seats,
While planets trade puns over cosmic treats.

In a universe where humor's the grace,
Astrophysics turns into a warming embrace.
So turn up the fun, let the humor unfold,
In this vast universe, stories are gold.

Celestial Caricatures

In the solar system, a sun wears a hat,
While Venus poses with a cat-astrophic spat.
Mercury zips by on a speedy flight,
Jupiter jokes, 'Don't take things too light!'

Mars draws faces on its dusty red hills,
Saturn's got rings that can give you the chills.
Uranus laughs hard at its own silly name,
Neptune just spins without any shame.

Galactic selfies are taken with flair,
Black holes complain there's too much to bear.
Stars wink and twinkle, joining the fun,
While satellites hum like a well-tuned pun.

In this cosmic art show, humor's the key,
With stars as the audience, come laugh with me.
Each quasar is bursting with comic delight,
In a universe filled with laughter so bright.

Jovial Jinxes

A quirky quasar dropped its shining crown,
While a planet spun round with a cheeky frown.
Stars play charades in a light-speed game,
While meteors tumble, igniting the flame.

A little dwarf planet took up the stage,
With jokes so corny, they turned the page.
Comets burst forth in a trail of delight,
Yodeling their way through the starlit night.

Wormholes whisper secrets of ancient lore,
Telling tales of space that we can't ignore.
Galaxies giggle at their spiral dance,
In this jinx of joy, give humor a chance.

So let's raise our glasses as stardust we drink,
And toast to the cosmos, forever in sync.
With laughter and light that time can't unpin,
In this wild universe, let the fun begin!

Celestial Cohorts

A moonlit rendezvous in the starry night,
With comets and clusters, everything's light.
Galaxies gathering for a cosmic feast,
While black holes take selfies, a moment's least.

Celestial buddies trading jokes and views,
While dust clouds dance with the stellar hues.
Every nebula glimmers with laughter anew,
As constellations gather, a warm cosmic brew.

Ringing meteors race through a silver sea,
While planets do pirouettes, wild and free.
In this celestial circus, the stars play their parts,
Creating a universe filled with joyful hearts.

So come join the dance in a twinkling ball,
Where laughter echoes and joy's for us all.
In this grand celestial theater, take your seat,
And let's share a chuckle, making life sweet!

Nebulae Nonsense

In the cloud of gas, a fart was found,
Asteroids laughed, making quite a sound.
Stars twinkled bright, like a disco ball,
While comets danced, having a ball!

Astro-bunnies on a cosmic run,
Chasing moonbeams, oh what fun!
Galactic giggles in the Milky Way,
As Saturn's rings began to sway.

Shooting stars wore silly hats,
Joking with meteors, just like chitchats.
Cosmic jesters trying to impress,
Weaving their humor through the vastness.

In this nonsensical starry flight,
Laughter echoes through the night.
Near the asteroid belt, a joke unfolds,
As gravity pulls, the fun never grows old.

Celestial Sibling Stories

Mars teased Earth, 'You look so blue!'
Earth shot back, 'Look who's red—you!'
Venus chimed in, 'Let's not bicker,
I shine so bright, I'm quite the sticker!'

Jupiter's storms, a swirling spree,
'Who'll clean this mess?' asked he with glee.
Uranus laughed, 'It's not my turn!'
'You made it worse, now we all learn!'

Neptune said, 'I'll bring ice cream!'
Yet Pluto's pout made him want to scream.
'You're not a planet, just a pet!'
Pluto smirked, 'But I'm the best yet!'

The cosmic siblings, full of jest,
Playing games, they are the best.
Around the Sun, they swirl and sway,
Sharing laughs in a bright ballet.

Interstellar Irony

Black holes pull, but it's all in jest,
'We're just vacuum cleaners, doing our best!'
Planets roll their eyes at such tales,
While asteroids jest like old-time gales.

Light-years fly, yet time stands still,
'This joke's so old, it gives me a thrill!'
Quasars wink, making light of their fate,
'We shine so bright, we can't hesitate!'

Aliens grinned, their ship was a wreck,
'We misread directions; we lack the tech!'
Yet each little mishap brought laughter so wide,
As they navigated the cosmos, side by side.

So here we are, in this vast void,
Finding the fun in what's been destroyed.
With irony wrapped in a stellar embrace,
We giggle and laugh in endless space.

Comedic Cosmos

Galaxies swirl in a joyous spin,
Comedic black holes, ready to win.
Stars have parties, throwing a bash,
While planets bump into each other with a crash!

Satellites sing, with tunes of delight,
'We're the backup dancers, shining so bright!'
Nebulae giggle, with colors ablaze,
Creating a canvas of humorous plays.

Meteor showers, a festive rain,
Dropping punchlines like a playful chain.
In the heart of the universe, all mixed up,
Even the farthest feel the light-hearted clap.

So let's toast to the cosmos, wild and free,
Where laughter and light are the key.
In this whimsical void, we take flight,
Crafting joy from the depths of the night.

Orbital Oddities

In a realm where moons wear hats,
Stars juggle as they chat.
Saturn's rings are fashion trends,
While comets race with lightning bends.

Asteroids dance in silly shoes,
Galaxies play hide and snooze.
Nebulas wear vibrant ties,
Cosmic laughter fills the skies.

Space whales swim through solar seas,
While Martians serve up cosmic teas.
Planets spin in joyful glee,
Creating quirks for all to see.

Astral Antics

In a picnic on a shooting star,
They barbecue from near and far.
Uranus claims the title of chef,
While Venus is the hostess left.

Jupiter tosses pies in flight,
Mars giggles at the sight.
Black holes play hide and seek,
While quasar jokes make them squeak.

A supernova sings a tune,
As stars wear shades beneath the moon.
Asteroids rock and bounce about,
In this cosmic giggle route.

Twinkle Twins

Two stars giggle as they twirl,
Spreading sparkles, watch them whirl.
They swap their places now and then,
Creating waves of joyous zen.

With cosmic crayons in their hands,
They doodle on the outer bands.
A constellation dressed in flair,
Catches laughter in the air.

They tell tales of spaceships bright,
With shiny sails that dance in flight.
The universe, their stage so grand,
As each joke echoes through the land.

Gravity of Jest

In a universe that takes a dip,
Jokes come floating, take a trip.
A comet slips on cosmic ice,
While gravity plays tricks, oh so nice.

Stars get tangled in their beams,
Dreams swirl like whirling streams.
Moonbeams tickle planets round,
As laughter with stardust is found.

Space-time folds, and twists, and bends,
Where every punchline never ends.
In galaxies where fun prevails,
Cosmos sings in joyful tales.

Extraterrestrial Exchanges

Two Martians walked into a bar,
One said, "Why so far?"
The other glanced at the moon,
"Just checking for a tune!"

When Venus joined in for a laugh,
She said, "I lost my other half!"
The guys all rolled their eyes,
"You know, that's no surprise!"

Jupiter gossiped with a ring,
"I hear Saturn has chickens to bring!"
But when they hit the dance floor,
They tripped over the meteor store!

So across the cosmic sea,
Humor flows so easily!
With aliens cracking jokes,
The universe just pokes!

Stellar Stand-up

A star on stage cracks a light pun,
"Why did Pluto never run?"
The crowd shrieked with delight,
"Cause he's always out of sight!"

Nearby, a comet joins the fun,
"I'm soft and ball of ice, not a gun!"
A planet chuckles, takes a spin,
"Well, that's how you lose your skin!"

Neptune jokes about his blues,
"I tried to get a job at the cruise!"
But the waves just swept him away,
"Gotta stay cool, it's my only way!"

As laughter echoes through the night,
Celestial beings bask in light,
With jokes orbiting like cosmic dust,
In this galaxy, humor is a must!

Comedic Constellation Chronicles

In the Big Dipper, laughter flows,
"Why do stars never lose?"
They all shine bright with their tricks,
"Because they know all the flicks!"

Down by Orion's belt so tight,
A joke about his weight takes flight,
"He's always packing a punch!"
"Or is that just a cosmic lunch?"

Cassiopeia sways with flair,
"I'm the queen, they all must stare!"
But her crown's a crescent moon,
"Don't forget my stellar tune!"

As asteroids tumble with glee,
Tickling comets that fly so free,
In this chronicle of spaced-out jest,
Universes laugh, we're truly blessed!

Outlandish Orbital Oddities

"What's green and travels far?"
"An alien in a candy car!"
Giggles ripple through the sky,
"Show me where you found that guy!"

A wormhole asks, "What's my role?"
"To stretch the truth and make it whole!"
The sun snickers, bright and bold,
"Just don't get too far from the gold!"

Uranus blushed when the jokes came,
"Why's my humor always the same?"
The crowd erupted in uproarious cheer,
"Because you've got nothing to fear!"

This quirky space where laughter reigns,
With jokes that soar like bouncing planes,
In oddities orbiting without a care,
Joyful banter fills the air!

Hypothetical Hilarity

In a world where cats wear hats,
And dogs play chess with chats,
Fish swim in shoes of light,
While birds take off in flight.

Jellybeans dance on moons,
With chocolate waves and tunes,
Squirrels discuss their nuts,
While robots argue in ruts.

A comet sips on tea,
As aliens shout with glee,
Pineapples climb the trees,
Wishing to float with ease.

Laughter echoes through the stars,
As spacemen race in candy cars,
In this land of silly sights,
Joy abounds on cosmic nights.

Cosmic Connections

Stars trade jokes through the void,
With laughter they are overjoyed,
A planet wears a silly grin,
While comets whirl and spin.

A fish flies high in the air,
Trading secrets without a care,
Meanwhile, clouds perform a dance,
As meteors get caught in a trance.

Nebulas joke about their flair,
As moons gossip with a dare,
Galaxies swirl with grinning glee,
In this cosmic jubilee.

Light-years vanish in this fun,
Where starlight plays and runs,
Every twinkle tells a tale,
Of joy upon this ethereal trail.

Tawdry Tidal Tales

On shores of laughter and glee,
Waves tickle the cosmic sea,
A crab wears a pirate's hat,
While seaweed dances with a cat.

Turtles surf the tidal wave,
Winking, oh so very brave,
Seagulls swoop with jokes to share,
In salty air, they float with flair.

Jellyfish perform a show,
As starfish steal the glow,
Barnacles with smirks so bright,
Join the fun under moonlight.

Countless tales from the deep,
Where laughter helps us leap,
In waters filled with joy and play,
Silly dreams come out to stay.

Tales from the Twilight Zones

In the twilight where shadows meet,
Mice wear capes and dance on feet,
While owls play chess with bees,
Giggling 'neath the bending trees.

A worm tells jokes from the ground,
As flocks of birds whirl around,
The moon snickers at the fun,
While stars begin to run.

Floating in a whirl of dreams,
Wormholes burst with silly beams,
Time gets tangled in a rhyme,
As laughter skips through space and time.

In the zones where whimsy thrives,
Imagination surely drives,
Endless tales of joy we find,
In these quirky worlds unconfined.

Starlit Shenanigans

In a galaxy where cows wear shades,
Stars plan pranks in cosmic cascades.
Mars tells jokes that leave comets reeling,
While Venus giggles at the whole feeling.

A spaceship pizza delivery's a hit,
With toppings that dance and never quite sit.
Asteroids throw a confetti parade,
While black holes are just tired of charades.

Interstellar games of hide and seek,
Saturn's rings pulling a youthful cheek.
Neptune's waltz makes everyone spin,
In this starlit realm, laughter's the win.

So swing on a comet, join in the fun,
This universe pranks till the day is done.
Lightyears of laughter, oh what a sight,
In a world where silly shines ever bright.

Cosmic Twinning

In the sky, two moons play a game,
One's quite shy, the other, quite lame.
They trade places just for a laugh,
While Jupiter giggles, doing the math.

Galaxies spin like twins in a whirl,
With nebulae dancing, giving a twirl.
Constellations gossip, sharing a wink,
While comets argue about who's in sync.

Asteroids tumble, attempting a roll,
While black holes gossip about their old soul.
Why did the star break up with its light?
It needed some space—what a cosmic plight!

So toast to the twinning and laughter galore,
With starry-eyed schemes, who could want more?
In this universe of doubles and puns,
The giggles echo where joy never shuns.

Dual Dimensions of Delight

In another realm, where shadows can talk,
Time takes a stroll, and space likes to walk.
Two suns having tea with a side of jam,
While a quirky comet sings, "I am who I am!"

Dimensions collide, and the fun's in full swing,
A planet called Giggle, where all creatures sing.
Chasing rainbows while wearing silly hats,
Life's but a jest with some cosmic spats.

Wormholes twist into spiral rides,
With noodles of starlight that tickle your sides.
If gravity falters, we just float around,
In this delightful dance with no need for ground.

Through loops and curves in a whimsical way,
Smiles echo brightly, brightening the day.
In dual dimensions, it's all quite absurd,
Where joy bursts forth, like a tickling bird.

Universe Unplugged

In this vast space, tuning is key,
Where jokes on the waves dance wild and free.
Asteroids jam in a rock and roll band,
With each boulder groove, they take a bold stand.

Galactic stand-up is quite the delight,
With stars telling tales each shimmering night.
Why did Mars refuse to break bread?
Too many craters—they went to his head!

In the vacuum, laughter bounces around,
Quantum giggles buoy the lost and found.
Uranus chuckles, with rings all a-sway,
In this cosmic satire, we all love to play.

So switch off the worry, malfunctions allowed,
Unplug from the fuss, let joy be avowed.
In a universe where humor takes flight,
The fun keeps in orbit, it's pure delight!

Jovian Jests

In Jupiter's storms, they'll always dive,
The clouds are thick but jokes survive.
They laugh through the thunder, joy in the air,
With swirling giggles, no need for a pair.

Saturn spins rings, a dazzling sight,
But check for the punchline, it's out of sight.
A comet's tail, with humor it trails,
As stars wink back, delight never fails.

In a moonlit circus, Uranus will sway,
With a tilt that's quirky, it steals the day.
Jokes orbit like satellites, laughter takes flight,
And glimmering stardust brings joy every night.

With cosmos' canvas, their antics so grand,
Ideas collide as they craft a new stand.
In the galaxy's theater, where giggles take root,
Their humor ignites, oh what a hoot!

Lunar Laugh Lines

On a crescent moon, a joke took a leap,
It tickled the stars, not a secret to keep.
They chuckle at aliens, what a fine show,
Their laughter resounds in the dark, soft glow.

Riding the tides, the oceans all sway,
With craters so deep, they hold jokes at bay.
A lunar eclipse, like laughter's fine pause,
Brought humor to light, and applause because.

With lunar landers that trip on their gear,
They send back a signal, "Hey! Come over here!"
The astronauts chuckle, each line is a draw,
"Just keep your toes light, and don't make a flaw!"

In twilight's embrace, the swirls start to dance,
With moonbeam routines, they offer a chance.
For laughter's the language in the dark, shining bright,
Under cosmic spotlight, everything feels right!

Timeless Twin Tales

In a twin star system, the jests never end,
One's a joker, the other a trend.
They swap silly stories, oh what a delight,
With lightyears of laughs that echo through night.

In the void, they trade gags, from dusk until dawn,
While shadows laugh lightly, two souls keep on.
Around every corner, a punchline revolves,
As cosmic twins puzzle and mystery solves.

Sitting on stardust, they share every scheme,
Creating a tapestry born from a dream.
With two minds together, they draw up the plan,
To tickle the universe, oh yes, they can!

As black holes may swallow, their joy stays intact,
The gravity's pull but a moment, not fact.
In a universe swirling, with humor in play,
The twins beam bright, as they giggle all day!

Nonconformist Nebulas

In a cloud of color, where oddities flock,
Nonconformist comets, they dance 'round the clock.
With whimsical shapes, they swirl in the breeze,
Crafting delightful spirals that tickle with ease.

Neon explosions, where laughter ignites,
Breaking the rules of conventional sights.
Galactic graffiti, jokes whispered in light,
In this vibrant realm, they take humor to flight.

On the fringes of chaos, they spin and they roll,
A nebula's heart hides a flickering soul.
With every new twist, the fun's in the chase,
In the cosmos of antics, there's room for each face.

So gather those chuckles, let giggles collide,
In the essence of stardust, let joy be your guide.
A universe teeming with whimsy and flair,
Nonconformist nebulas, where laughter is rare!

Space-Savvy Satire

In cosmos' game of hide and seek,
The stars wear socks, not quite unique.
Mercury's swift but takes a nap,
While Jupiter's got an interstellar trap.

Venus threw a party so divine,
With dancing comets and space-age wine.
Mars brought snacks, a tasty delight,
But the robots danced all through the night.

The Sun, the host, with radiant flair,
Told black holes to stop with their glare.
Asteroids juggled in jovial jest,
While aliens debated who's the best.

So grab your telescope, peek through the view,
In this cosmic circus, there's fun for you!
With every quirk in the vast expanse,
The universe winks with a twinkling dance.

Whimsical Worlds Apart

On a world where cats wear hats,
And dogs can chat like chubby brats.
The skies rain cheese, oh what a dream,
While penguins slide with a silly scream.

Zebras paint stripes in polka dots,
As hippos play chess in muddy spots.
Clouds are made of cotton candy,
And candy canes grow ever handy.

Balloons fly high with witty tales,
As rabbits cruise in tiny gales.
Each land a riddle wrapped in fun,
Where laughter brightens every sun.

So let your heart drift on this whim,
Where everything quirky is not too grim.
In the worlds apart, joy never fails,
And imagination sets its sails.

Astrological Alter Egos

Capricorn grumbles, loves his rules,
While Gemini juggles a pool of fools.
Leo roars loud in a lion's den,
But Cancer just wants to chill with friends.

Aquarius dreams of a techie fate,
Pisces swims deep, in thoughts they bait.
Aries races, can't stand to wait,
While Virgo scorns in meticulous state.

Sagittarius shoots for the stars so high,
Libra's at peace, still wondering why.
Taurus munches, keeps it real,
But Scorpio's secrets are part of the deal.

In this cosmic cast, the roles are clear,
Stars align with a touch of cheer.
Though egos clash in astral delight,
We'll laugh and dance through stars every night.

Quasar Quips

Quasars giggle in cosmic light,
With truths so deep, they spark delight.
Wormholes hide jokes beneath their wraps,
As galaxies spin in clever laps.

A quasar's wink sends comets whirling,
While neutron stars keep the laughter curling.
The milky way plays jokes on black holes,
As quasars share secrets with shopping trolls.

Between the voids, puns fly around,
In the echo of silence, laughter's found.
Stars collaborate, in the vast unknown,
Crafting humor, a universal tone.

So tune your radar to interstellar fun,
Unravel the jokes from worlds yet to run.
In this cosmic jest, there's always more,
With every pun, watch the universe roar.

Intergalactic Improv

In a galaxy far, jokes collide,
Planets spin, humor won't hide.
Aliens laugh, their eyes a-glow,
While earthlings miss the punchline show.

Astronauts dance on cosmic air,
With solar flares to spare a care.
Laughter rockets, bright and bold,
Tickling stars, a sight to behold.

Neptune cracked a witty pun,
As Saturn laughed, oh what fun!
Even black holes join the cheer,
Gulping gags from far and near.

In this vast space of soaring wit,
Stellar banter, each tiny bit.
So if you drift near a comet's tail,
Be ready for a cosmic tale!

Comets' Comedy Corners

Comets zoom with jokes galore,
Tail feathers tickle, never a bore.
Meteorites join in the jest,
While asteroids ponder their best.

In the comedy club of the skies,
Stars trade puns with twinkling eyes.
A supernova bursts with glee,
While space dust laughs so carelessly.

Galactic giggles spin like a kite,
As black holes gulp down laughter light.
The universe chuckles, no need to frown,
In Comets' Corner, no one wears a crown.

Cosmic clowns with an orbiting twist,
Dodging humor like a surrealist.
Join the show, the laughter's grand,
In this corner of the starry band.

Star-Crossed Satire

Star-crossed lovers meet in jest,
Planets joke, they feel so blessed.
They parry jokes across the void,
With every punchline, tensions toyed.

Mars says, 'Your orbit's quite absurd!'
Venus laughs and calls him 'bird.'
Each witty remark breaks the ice,
In love's vast space, all things are nice.

Galaxies giggle, galaxies tease,
While cosmic winds rustle the trees.
In the expanse, nothing's too serious,
Just bright banter, nothing too curious.

Starlight snapshots capture the fun,
In a stellar ballet, all pun is spun.
So cherish these jesters of the cosmos high,
With humor as vast as the evening sky.

Starlight Shenanigans

Under starlight, where mischief breeds,
Cosmic jokesters plant their seeds.
They spin tales of whimsical delight,
While pulsars wink in the silver night.

Wormholes twist with quirky grace,
Laughter echoes through time and space.
As quasars beam their radiant light,
The universe joins in, sparkling bright.

Shooting stars weave a funny spree,
While galaxies dance in harmony.
In this playground of cosmic fun,
Even the void knows how to run.

So gather your friends, celestial and wide,
Embrace the laughter, let joy be your guide.
In the grand scheme of starlit charms,
Join in the shenanigans, love's warm arms.

Saturnine Satires

On Saturn's rings, a hula hoop spins,
With aliens dancing, oh where to begin?
Jupiter's jealous, his storms in a swirl,
'Cause Saturn's so stylish, in a cosmic twirl.

Venus tried fashion, but the heat's just too bold,
While Mars claims his rovers find treasures of gold.
Pluto feels left out, just a dwarf in the fray,
But makes a grand joke, 'Hey, I'm still on display!'

Neptune's fishing tales are truly a catch,
While Mercury's racing, can't find a good match.
Galileo chuckles as he gazes afar,
In a sea of giggles brought on by a star.

With comets that wink and a cheeky moonbeam,
Astronauts laugh till they burst at the seam.
In the cosmic playground, we'll frolic and run,
For the galaxy's humor is never outdone.

Laughter Amid the Stars

In the Milky Way's laugh track, stars shine so bright,
They giggle at comets that zoom in the night.
Orion's got jokes, but they're lost in the lore,
As he battles the urge to hit the floor.

Black holes are moody, don't take them for fun,
They'll swallow your punchlines, and still want to run.
But on the moon's surface, with craters like pies,
Laughter erupts under wide-open skies.

The sun cracks a joke, 'Why did Mars turn red?'
'Cause he saw Venus and wished he were wed!'
In a galaxy where puns add a twist,
Cosmic giggles emerge, no moment is missed.

Asteroids tumble, their paths full of cheer,
Each collision a joke, hearty laughter we hear.
With rings of delight, the planets align,
In this vast universe, where humor will shine.

Celestial Reflections

In a cosmic mirror, reflections abound,
With Martian mirth echoing all around.
Venus laughs lightly, her clouds in a spin,
While Saturn whispers, 'Let the games begin!'

Stars twinkle with glee, each with a delight,
Playing tag with the moons in the warmth of the night.
What do you call a black hole that sings?
A stellar performer, it simply brings bling.

In a galaxy of giggles, the nebula sways,
With humor that stretches through eons and days.
The sun holds a pun, brightening the gloom,
Saying, 'Shine on, folks, there's always more room!'

With laughter like stardust, we tumble and twirl,
In the cosmic dance, all our worries unfurl.
So raise up your voice, let the echoes resound,
In this universe, joy is always around.

Cosmic Doppelgängers

Look at that Martian, he's sporting a hat,
Announcing to Earth, 'I'm where it's at!'
Jupiter chuckles, 'I'm the leader of tones,'
As his moons mimic laughter with jovial groans.

In a parallel world, Neptune wears specs,
As he reads all the jokes that the cosmos collects.
Pluto's a pop star, in a galactic band,
With songs full of puns that go hand in hand.

Mirror worlds doubling, oh what a sight,
Where aliens burst forth with jokes, pure delight.
The stars play a game of cosmic charades,
With laughter that echoes in silvery shades.

So gather your friends, from this space-time ride,
Find joy among planets where giggles abide.
In galaxies beyond, where humor unfolds,
A universe of laughter, more precious than gold.

Cosmic Curiosities

In a universe filled with quirk,
A star tried to dance, went berserk.
It twirled with a comet, oh so bold,
But ended up wrapped in a space blanket of gold.

Black holes in the kitchen, quite a sight,
They suck in crumbs, with pure delight.
While aliens BBQ on a distant moon,
Their grilling skills? A cosmic cartoon.

Supernova spaghetti, oh what a mess,
Asteroids tossing, creating stress.
In this odd world where oddities thrive,
The laughter of stardust keeps us alive.

Galaxies giggle, and planets play tag,
In this vast cosmos, nothing's a drag.
So next time you stargaze under the night,
Remember the punchlines that bring pure delight.

Galactic Giggles

In a nebula where laughter blooms,
Jokes orbit like planets, banishing gloom.
A satellite squeaks with a playful jest,
Broadcasting humor, the universe's best.

Comets chase each other, racing through space,
Telling old tales, they quicken their pace.
With each cosmic chuckle, they leave a trace,
Creating a ring of joy in a vast embrace.

Asteroids chuckling, rolling down hills,
Their rocky laughter gives us the thrills.
While the Milky Way winks, it's hard not to see,
How funny the cosmos can truly be!

From Martian musings to lunar puns,
Every star twinkles while bursting with funs.
So shout to the heavens, let laughter ignite,
In this whimsical galaxy, everything's bright!

Orbital Oaths

Stars with vows to keep the laughs flowing,
Swore to lighten up while the cosmos keeps glowing.
They pledged to giggle 'till dark becomes light,
Holding hands in the silence of night.

When Venus sings, her notes float afar,
Earth joins the chorus, a celestial star.
Their melodies mingle like sugar and spry,
Making sure every heart has a reason to fly.

Planets take turns in a dizzying waltz,
Throwing out puns with delightful faults.
From Jupiter's jokes to Saturn's sly grin,
Each orbital promise starts from within.

So gather your stardust, let's all unite,
In the galactic oath to laugh at the night.
For in every twinkle and each cosmic beam,
Lies the promise of joy that fuels our dream.

Twin Star Shenanigans

Twin stars twinkle in cosmic embrace,
Playing pranks on the comets that race.
One sings a tune while the other does the dance,
Together they giggle in a stellar romance.

They whispered to Earth, 'What's life like there?'
And received a reply, 'Full of chaos and flair!'
With each silly jest, they brighten the void,
Turning dark space into humor enjoyed.

Zipping through orbits, they make quite the team,
Filling the night with their light-hearted scheme.
Meteor showers become laugh-filled rains,
These twins remind us that joy never wanes.

So if you see lights that dance in the sky,
Know that it's laughter, going by with a sigh.
For in this vast universe where oddities play,
The twins keep us laughing, come night or day!

Constellation Capers

In the night sky, stars are bright,
They twinkle and dance, what a sight!
Orion's lost his belt, oh dear,
I guess it's laundry day, I fear.

The Big Dipper spills drinks on the moon,
While the Little Bear hums a tune.
And if you ask the Milky Way,
She just laughs, 'It's a cosmic café!'

Comets race at the speed of light,
Playing tag with the planets, what a fright!
Venus says, "I'm hotter than you!"
While Mars just rolls his eyes, it's true.

Saturn's rings spin in a whirl,
While Jupiter twirls, giving a twirl.
Aliens peek through for a glance,
At this stellar, humorous dance!

Starlit Satires

In a nebula, wacky laughs abound,
Jokes floating in space, no solid ground.
Uranus giggles, "Not my fault!"
As Earth just sighs and starts to halt.

The rockets zoom with engines loud,
While Pluto claims, "I'm still proud!"
A dwarf planet willing to jest,
Yet they laugh, "At least I'm the best!"

Eclipses hide behind shadows of fun,
As sunbeams play with everyone.
A solar flare tickles the night,
Making satellites giggle in flight.

Black holes burp with cosmic glee,
Swallowing stars in a raucous spree.
In this galaxy of chuckles and quirks,
Laughter echoes where humor lurks.

Galactic Gleanings

On distant worlds, oddities thrive,
With creatures who dance and jive.
Space cows moo in zero-gravity,
While robot sheep sing with levity.

Mars threw a party, oh what a blast!
But Venus crashed, arriving last.
She sighed, "Traffic through space is wild!"
As comets laughed, spinning and styled.

The Andromeda strain's nothing but cheer,
With beings who laugh, spreading good cheer.
Galaxies swirl in a comedic spin,
While asteroids laugh, "Can we join in?"

Time travels wacky, bending all rules,
With paradox parties for quirky fools.
In this universe of fun and jest,
Every joke shared is a cosmic quest!

Universe of Utter Absurdity

Stars wear hats from a thrift store pick,
While moons play cards, oh what a trick!
Shooting stars fall, making wishes frail,
But they just giggle, "We'll still prevail!"

Neptune's blues sing the saddest tunes,
While space whales dance to the light of moons.
A supernova bursts into laughter bright,
Lighting up the void, a stunning sight.

Aliens toast to life with green jelly,
While space contorts like a playful belly.
Asteroids juggle, trying not to drop,
While black holes spin with a cosmic hop.

In this universe of twinkling glee,
Join in the laughter, come see, come see!
With each absurdity shared from afar,
We find joy together, no matter how bizarre!

Celestial Comedy Tour

The stars align with giggles bright,
A Neptune jester takes to flight.
With rings that sparkle, laughter flies,
While Martian friends sing silly cries.

Through cosmic jokes and starry smiles,
We roam the void for endless miles.
A comet's tail, a tail of fun,
In this expanse, we're never done!

Asteroids roll, they trip and fall,
Their rocky cries, the funniest call.
Black holes laugh, they've got no shame,
In this vast space, we play the game.

Galactic gigs, now that's the goal,
With alien acts that steal the show!
Each cosmic laugh becomes a song,
In this grand tour, we all belong.

Comet Comedy Cabaret

In the cosmic club, the comets dance,
With jokes that spin and stars in a trance.
Uranus plays the sax, so cool,
While Venus cracks jokes, breaking the rule.

Saturn's rings spin tales of glee,
As Martians cheer, "Hey, look at me!"
The meteors drop, they steal the scene,
With puns so bright, they glimmer and gleam.

Galactic giggles echo through the night,
Asteroid barflies sipping starlight.
They wobble and sway with classic flair,
And space-time laughs bounce everywhere.

Galaxies cheer for this starry bash,
With comets soaring, making a splash.
Join the fun, don't miss the show,
Where laughter echoes through space's flow.

Improbable Intergalactic Insights

In cosmic realms of wild delight,
Where insights shine like stars at night.
Jupiter muses with a cosmic wink,
"Why do planets always think?"

Venus giggles, "It's all a blur,
Why do aliens always purr?"
With laughter bright and thoughts so bold,
In this galactic tale, all is gold.

With wormholes twisting every way,
We ponder life in our own way.
The universe winks, a clever tease,
Reflecting thoughts with cosmic ease.

Stars reveal their quirky plots,
With jokes that weave in cosmic knots.
Black holes hum with wise old song,
In this interstellar laugh, we all belong.

Mystic Moonbeam Mischief

Under moonlight, the antics start,
With moonbeams playing a cheeky part.
Lunar giggles, a playful scene,
As shadows dance and shine serene.

The craters chuckle, deep and round,
Where echoes of laughter do abound.
In mystic nights, the jokes take flight,
Whispers of humor in the night.

Punny riddles bounce from star to star,
As nighttime critters drive the car.
Space-frogs leap with a ribbit or two,
While cosmic cats paint skies so blue.

Join the fun in this moonlit spree,
With comets passing, oh so free.
For in this mischief, joy ignites,
Where laughter reigns throughout the nights.

Twin Peaks of Wit

Two mountains stand firm, side by side,
One says, "I'm taller, come take a ride!"
The other just laughs, "You're full of hot air,
But I'll summit with style, if you just dare!"

In valleys of giggles, they poke fun anew,
"Your shadows are shorter, it's clear, it's true!"
While climbers just pause, scratching their heads,
As peaks exchange jokes, and wisdom spreads.

Life's uphill battles with laughter embrace,
Scaling the heights of the mountain's grace.
With every step up, a pun takes its flight,
As echoes of laughter ring out through the night.

At the summit they meet, a grand joke-telling spree,
Where nature's comedians break into glee.
With stones as their audience, they share in delight,
Two peaks with a punchline, gleeful and bright!

Celestial Chuckles

Stars twinkle and wink, cozy in space,
"Did you hear that one? It's a real big grace!"
The moon grins down, glowing in delight,
"I'm the king of night jokes, hold on tight!"

A comet zooms by with a blast of a laugh,
"Why was the planet not good at math?"
Everyone chuckles, but the sun can't see,
"I'm too busy shining, come laugh with me!"

Nebulas swirl, knitting tales in the dark,
Each story a spark, each laugh like a lark.
"Why did the astronaut break up with her guy?
She needed more space; oh, me, oh my!"

In galactic gatherings, the fun never ends,
Cosmic comedians sharing jokes with their friends.
Floating on laughter, drifting through stars,
The universe chuckles, from Venus to Mars!

Moonbeam Misunderstandings

Once on a night with a silvery glow,
The moon shined bright, but tripped on a toe!
"Is that a crater?" it asked in surprise,
As a shooting star winked, with twinkling eyes.

"Why don't scientists trust their moonlit tales?"
"Because they're often full of meteoric fails!"
A comet rolled laughing through the dark sky,
"At least we can travel, we're always nearby!"

But, when shadows danced in a playful way,
The sun couldn't resist, joined in on the play.
"I might be bright, but you've got the wit!
Let's ride this light cycle, let's give it a hit!"

Together they crafted a jest of delight,
A moon and a sun, a puzzling sight.
In the glow of the darkness, giggles took flight,
As stars gathered 'round for a laugh-filled night!

Cosmic Conundrums

In the galaxy wide, strange riddles reside,
Planets exchange whispers, laughter their guide.
"Why did the dwarf planet feel so small?"
"Because it was once king, now it's just tall!"

Asteroids chuckle, spinning along,
Clashing in humor, where all jokes belong.
"What's a black hole's favorite wordless spree?"
"To suck in the fun—come play with me!"

With every rotation, the universe spins,
Jokes travel fast, and the laughter begins.
"Why did the star break up with the sky?
Too much pressure to shine, oh my, oh my!"

Through nebula clouds, with giggles to share,
Celestial beings float everywhere.
In the cosmos' embrace, the puns intertwine,
Living in harmony, all laughter divine!

Mirrored Moons

In a world where shadows play,
The moons giggle night and day.
One says, 'I'm full of cheese!'
The other shouts, 'Oh, please!'

They sway in a dance of light,
Mistaken for a cosmic fright.
One moon says, 'I've lost my glow!'
The other beams, 'It's just for show!'

With craters making funny faces,
They share jokes from different places.
A comet zips by with a grin,
Saying, 'Come on, let the fun begin!'

Lunar laughter fills the skies,
As they tease stars with silly lies.
In this mirrored cosmic room,
The moons are the masters of their boom!

Eclipsed Echoes

Two suns share a silly chat,
One's too bright, the other's flat.
They joke about their burning fate,
'You shine, I just radiate!'

In shadows where the giggles clash,
Light dims down in a playful splash.
'Why'd you bring the eclipse today?'
'Because I wanted a darker play!'

Their rays collide in a wink,
'Hey, do you ever stop to think?'
'Only when I need to tan!'
'Well that's a solar master plan!'

A solar wind takes off the veil,
As laughter rides, like a comet's tail.
In shadows deep, the echoes play,
While suns abound in bright dismay!

Galaxy of Gags

In a cosmos vast and wide,
Galaxies swirl in a jolly ride.
One says, 'What's that glowing star?'
The other laughs, 'That's my car!'

They spin around with light and cheer,
Telling tales that all can hear.
'Got a riddle from the black hole?'
'Only if it's got a funny roll!'

Nebulae shimmer with delight,
Dancing through the starry night.
A supernova struts and brags,
'Bet you wish you had my tags!'

In this galaxy of jest and fun,
Laughter rockets, never done.
With cosmic puns and stellar glee,
The universe is one big comedy!

Cosmic Clones

Two comets met in a cosmic race,
One exclaimed, 'You've got my face!'
They laughed and twirled in space ballet,
Both thinking, 'What a stellar day!'

'Is that a tail or just a plume?'
'Nah, it's the latest cosmic loom!'
They threaded stars with jokes of old,
In a tapestry that's bold and gold.

Planetary friends join the fun,
Offering puns, one by one.
'Why did the asteroid fall apart?'
'Because it lost its shooting star heart!'

In cosmic twists, their laughter spins,
As echoes ring from quasar fins.
In this realm of silly clones,
Unity thrives in playful tones!

www.ingramcontent.com/pod-product-compliance
Lightning Source LLC
Chambersburg PA
CBHW051644160426
43209CB00004B/788